Cornerstones of Freedom

The National Mall

BRENDAN JANUARY

CHILDREN'S PRESS®
A Division of Grolier Publishing
New York • London • Hong Kong • Sydney
Danbury, Connecticut

Visit Children's Press on the Internet at:
http://publishing.grolier.com

Library of Congress Cataloging-in-Publication Data

January, Brendan, 1972–
    The National Mall / Brendan January.
       p. cm.—(Cornerstones of freedom)
    Includes index.
    Summary: Describes the history of the National Mall, the buildings
around it, and the special events that have been held there.
    ISBN 0-516-21616-3 (lib. bdg.)   0-516-27167-9 (pbk.)
    1. Mall, the (Washington, D.C.)—History—Juvenile literature.
2. Washington (D.C.)—Buildings, structures, etc.—Juvenile literature.
[1. Mall, The (Washington, D.C.) 2. National parks and reserves.]
I. Title. II. Series.
F203.5.M2 J36   2000
975.3—dc21
                                                    99-052349

In the 1950s and early 1960s, a civil rights leader named Martin Luther King Jr. battled tirelessly for the rights of African-Americans in the United States. For almost ten years, he led protests in the southern states. Then, in 1963, King planned to take his cause to a place where people across the United States could see and listen to him.

Martin Luther King Jr. delivers his "I Have a Dream" speech.

He decided to lead a march to the nation's capital, Washington, D.C. By late August 1963, more than 200,000 people had arrived. No building in the city could hold such a crowd. Instead, the leaders of the march directed people to gather on a long, rectangular park at the center of the city—the National Mall. On August 28, King stood on the steps of the Lincoln Memorial, gazed out over the crowd, and gave an eloquent and electrifying speech.

"I have a dream!" he cried, "that one day this nation will rise up and live out the true meaning of its creed: 'We hold these truths to be self-evident, that all men are created equal.'"

His words reminded the nation that the first sentence of the Declaration of Independence did not yet hold true for every American. Members of Congress saw the people rallying on the Mall and supporting equality. King's now-famous "I Have a Dream" speech contributed to the passage of the Civil Rights Act in 1964.

Why did King choose the Mall? What was so important about this place?

Washington is filled with government buildings where men and women make important decisions. North of the Mall, the president of the United States lives in the White House. To the east stands the stately Capitol building, where the Congress meets. Behind the Capitol, the Supreme Court listens to arguments about the nation's laws. But, as the March on Washington showed, open space can be more important than any elegant building. On the Mall, Americans can meet and debate the critical issues that face the nation.

Millions of people also visit the Mall to enjoy themselves. Surrounded by museums, monuments, and government buildings, the Mall is a majestic open space dotted with trees and lakes. Festivals take place there regularly. Every year on the Fourth of July, crowds watch a celebration of colorful fireworks lighting up the sky over the Washington Monument.

A Lincoln Memorial
B Vietnam Veterans Memorial
C Vietnam Women's Memorial
D Korean War Veterans Memorial
E Franklin Delano Roosevelt Memorial
F Thomas Jefferson Memorial
G White House
H Washington Monument
I U.S. Holocaust Memorial Museum
J National Museum of American History
K National Museum of Natural History
L Smithsonian Institution
M Hirshhorn Museum and Sculpture Garden
N National Gallery of Art, West Building
O National Air and Space Museum
P National Gallery of Art, East Building
Q U.S. Capitol
R Supreme Court

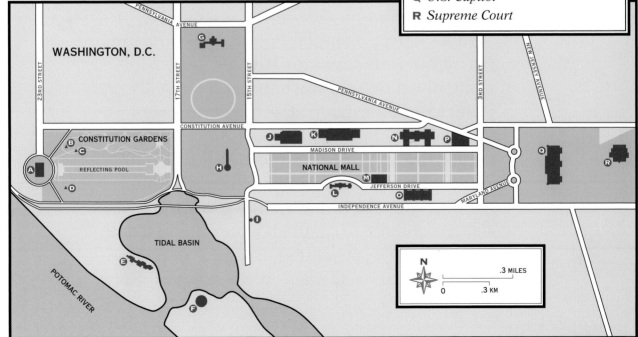

*Pierre Charles
L'Enfant*

Neither the city of Washington, D.C., nor the Mall existed in 1783, when the United States won its independence from Great Britain. Back then, the capital of the new country was in New York City. In that bustling northern port, George Washington was sworn in as the nation's first president in 1789. Many Americans, however, disapproved of the capital's location. In the South, people grumbled that New York City was too far away from the southern states. They feared that northerners would control the new government.

Led by Thomas Jefferson, southern leaders convinced Congress to build a new capital city on the border between Maryland and Virginia. In 1791, Congress hired Pierre Charles L'Enfant, a brilliant French architect and engineer, to design the city. The chosen site sat near the Potomac River.

About a mile from the Potomac stood a low, grassy hill called Jenkins Hill. On June 28, 1791, L'Enfant led George Washington to the hill's crest. Here, L'Enfant explained, is the perfect spot for a magnificent building for the Congress—the Capitol. West of the Capitol site, gently rolling fields ended at the Potomac River. L'Enfant planned to make this area into a "Grand Avenue, 400 feet in breadth, and about a mile in length, bordered with gardens, ending in a slope from the houses on each side." At the heart of this open, grassy space, L'Enfant envisioned a monument to his hero—George Washington.

Years later, L'Enfant's "Grand Avenue" would become the National Mall. On the northern side of the Mall, L'Enfant wanted to widen a creek into a canal—called Tiber Canal—that would carry boatloads of goods into the center of the city. North of the Mall, L'Enfant planned to build a "palace" for the president. This idea eventually became the White House. Plans for wide avenues and tree-lined parks filled L'Enfant's head. He dreamed of a capital that would rival the greatest cities in Europe, such as Paris and London.

But construction of Washington, D.C., took time. When L'Enfant died in 1825, the capital city was still rough and unfinished. Although the White House and the Capitol were built, many of the city's roads were unpaved and turned to mud when it rained. Ramshackle houses surrounded the large government buildings. To the west of the Capitol, the Mall was little more than wild, overgrown fields and swamps. L'Enfant's idea for a "Grand Avenue" was slowly forgotten.

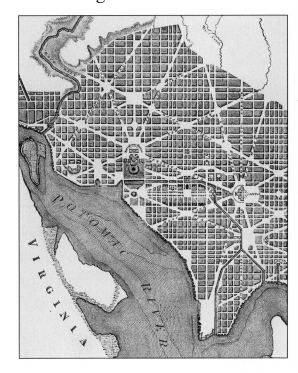

L'Enfant's plan of Washington, D.C., shows that in the late 1700s, the Potomac River covered much of the area that is now the western end of the National Mall.

James Smithson

In 1848, however, citizens began fulfilling the architect's dream of a monument on the Mall to the nation's first president, George Washington. After holding a design contest, a citizen organization selected a plan for a towering obelisk made of marble and granite. Construction began in 1848. Soon, people hoped, the National Mall would have its first monument.

Another change came to the Mall in the 1850s, and strangely enough, it came from a man who had never set foot in the United States. A wealthy British scientist—James Smithson— was inspired by the government in the United States. When Smithson died in 1829, he left his entire fortune to the new country. In his will, he wrote that the money should be used "to found in Washington, under the name Smithsonian Institution, an establishment for the increase and diffusion of knowledge among men."

In 1838, Smithson's fortune—105 bags of gold coins worth about $500,000—arrived in the capital city. But Congress couldn't agree on how to use the money. For several years, they argued over the matter. Finally, in 1846, former president John Quincy Adams suggested that the funds be used to build a museum. Congress agreed and ordered construction of the Smithsonian Institution to begin at once on the National Mall.

The Smithsonian Institution opened in 1855. Constructed of red sandstone and bristling with towers and battlements, it was soon known as "the Castle." Several hundred yards to the west, the base of the unfinished Washington Monument rose out of the fields. Andrew Jackson Downing, a man who loved plants and flowers, designed a series of gardens around the Castle. He laid out gently sloping paths and roads that wandered over the Mall. It was beautiful, but still a far cry from L'Enfant's flat, open "Grand Avenue."

The original Smithsonian Institution, or "the Castle." In front of the building is a statue of Joseph Henry, the first secretary of the Smithsonian.

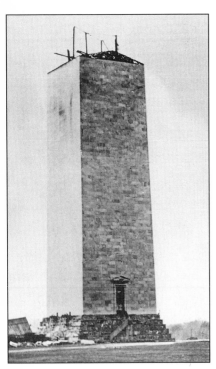

The unfinished Washington Monument in 1876

In the late 1850s, the United States was divided over the issue of slavery. In 1861, when Abraham Lincoln became president, the festering problem exploded into war between the North (the Union) and the South (the Confederacy). The American Civil War lasted four bloody years (1861–1865). Construction on the Washington Monument—already delayed—was abruptly halted. No one had the time to worry about the monument.

After the war ended in Union victory, people could again turn to the city's problems. In the 1870s, workmen filled in Tiber Canal and paved it over, transforming it into Constitution Avenue. Instead of a waterway carrying boats, L'Enfant's canal became a roadway transporting wagons, cars, and trucks. Today, a tiny stone house still stands alone on the Mall next to Constitution Avenue. During the mid-1800s, this small cottage was the lockkeeper's house (the house of the man who controlled the waterway). The structure is a small reminder that, at one time, there was a canal on the Mall.

The unfinished Washington Monument was still an eyesore. Congress voted funds for the project, and work on it resumed in 1878. Six years later, in 1884, workers installed a small pyramid of solid aluminum on the top. At a cost of $1,187,710, the Washington Monument was finally finished. More than 36,000 blocks of granite and marble, weighing more than 80,000 tons, make up the structure.

The lockkeeper's house was built in 1835.

A few years later, workmen installed a steam-powered elevator to take people to the top. The elevator operator allowed only men into the car, because the ride was considered too dangerous for women. If women wanted to see the view from the top of the 555-foot (169-m) tall monument, they had to climb the 897 stairs.

In 1900, however, the view of the Mall from the top of the monument was still anything but pleasant. The city of Washington had many splendid homes and avenues, but sheds and roughly built houses cluttered the Mall's open space. Several train tracks crossed the grounds, leading to an area of warehouses and railroad yards. Hundreds of acres of marsh had been filled in with soil along the Potomac River, extending the Mall another several hundred yards. But no one had landscaped it.

This photograph was taken in the mid-1940s. The U.S. Navy installed these temporary buildings on the Mall during World War II (1941–1945).

In 1900, Senator James McMillan organized a commission to study the city's park system. Two years later, he issued a plan that urged a return to L'Enfant's original idea for the Mall. Workmen soon removed a train station and other buildings that had cluttered the area, and the Mall began to look better. Still, the improvements took time, and national emergencies, such as wars, temporarily stopped the beautification of the Mall.

In 1911, a group of citizens won the support to build a memorial to Abraham Lincoln. As the leader who ended slavery and guided the nation through the Civil War, Lincoln was considered by many to be the greatest American president. The group selected a spot on the bank of the Potomac River on the west end of the Mall.

After twelve years and $3 million, the Lincoln Memorial was finished. More than fifty thousand people came to the dedication in 1922. The architect modeled the memorial after the Parthenon, a Greek temple. On the outside, thirty-six columns ring three giant chambers built of limestone, granite, and marble. Inside the central chamber, a seated, thoughtful statue of Lincoln looks out over the Mall.

Workers also began digging a "reflecting pool,"

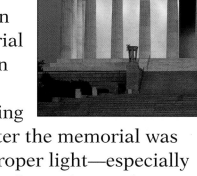

more than a third of a mile long, between the Lincoln Memorial and the Washington Monument. They finished the Reflecting Pool a few years after the memorial was dedicated. In the proper light—especially at night—the pool reflects the Washington Monument. From the Lincoln Memorial, visitors can enjoy a spectacular view of the Washington Monument and the Capitol dome.

The thirty-six columns of the Lincoln Memorial represent the thirty-six states of the Union at the time of Lincoln's death.

After the Lincoln Memorial was built, many people agreed that the National Mall was becoming a splendid space at the heart of the nation. It was also becoming a place where people could make their opinions known. In 1939, the famous African-American opera singer, Marian Anderson, planned to give a concert in Washington, D.C. When she tried to appear at Constitution Hall—the best concert hall in the city—the owners refused to give her permission to perform there because she was black. First Lady Eleanor Roosevelt, infuriated by the decision, helped arrange for Anderson to sing at the Lincoln Memorial. On Easter Sunday, 75,000 people gathered on the Mall to hear her concert. It is remembered as an important moment in the movement toward equal rights for African-Americans.

Marian Anderson

The Mall was the scene of other protests and demonstrations. In 1965, President Lyndon B. Johnson began to send thousands of young men to fight in a small Asian country called Vietnam. Most Americans had never questioned the U.S. involvement in earlier wars in Europe, Japan, and Korea. But Vietnam was different. When American soldiers began to die and suffer wounds in alarming numbers, protests erupted throughout the nation. To urge the president and the Congress to stop the war, people gathered on the Mall. Signs reading "Stop the Fighting" and "Bring the Boys Home" bobbed above the crowds. They sang songs and chanted slogans.

The last U.S. troops left Vietnam in 1975. After years of fighting, almost 60,000 Americans had

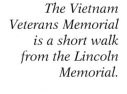

The Vietnam Veterans Memorial is a short walk from the Lincoln Memorial.

been killed. At home, the angry protests divided American society. Some people thought the government should have kept fighting. Others blamed the government for sending thousands of young men to their deaths.

In 1982, the war in Vietnam brought Americans to the Mall again. This time, however, they gathered to dedicate the Vietnam Veterans Memorial. The monument looks simple. On two, long rows of black granite panels, name after name is listed—almost 59,000. Each name is that of an American who died in Vietnam or who remains missing. The National Mall, once the scene of furious protests against the Vietnam War, is now a place where the war's veterans are honored.

The bronze statue of the three nurses is 7 feet (2.1 m) tall.

The names of eight women are also inscribed on the Wall. In 1988, a woman named Diane Carlson Evans won approval from Congress to erect a statue near the Wall honoring the women who served in Vietnam. The Vietnam Women's Memorial—dedicated on Veteran's Day in 1993—depicts three nurses, one of them tending a wounded soldier. Eight trees are planted around the statue in memory of the eight women who died in Vietnam.

The Korean War Memorial statues

Other veterans have erected monuments on the Mall. The Korean War Veterans Memorial honors the American soldiers who fought in Korea from 1950 to 1953. More than thirty thousand Americans died. Built in the shadow of the Lincoln Memorial and dedicated in 1995, the monument is unlike any other on the Mall. Nineteen stainless steel sculptures of U.S. soldiers trudge though a rough landscape of granite slabs and small bushes. The men appear tense and anxious, as if bullets could hit them at any moment. Nearby, granite walls tell more about the war. More than 2,400 pictures of men and women veterans are etched in one wall. Another declares: "Freedom Is Not Free."

The statue of Franklin Delano Roosevelt weighs approximately 1,500 pounds (680 kg). The statue of Fala weighs approximately 225 pounds (102 kg).

Near the Korean War Veterans Memorial is the Franklin Delano Roosevelt Memorial, which honors the thirty-second president. As president of the United States, Roosevelt guided the nation through the Great Depression of the 1930s and World War II (1939–1945). The memorial, completed in 1997, is a park of trees, waterfalls, and four galleries made of a red-colored granite. As visitors walk through the memorial, they see scenes illustrating how Roosevelt led the nation and life in America during his presidency. In the third room, a massive 8' 7.5" (2.63 meters) statue of Roosevelt sits in a chair, most of it covered in the folds of his cape. His Scottish terrier, Fala, stands alertly at the president's side. Quotes from his speeches are inscribed into the walls, including one of his most famous: "The only thing we have to fear is fear itself."

Roosevelt is one of four presidents honored on or near the Mall. The other three are Washington, Lincoln, and Thomas Jefferson. A memorial to Jefferson was built south of the Mall and dedicated in 1943. In the elegant domed memorial, a 19-foot (5.8-m) bronze statue of Jefferson stands on a 6-foot (1.8-m) pedestal. Inscriptions of Jefferson's writings, including passages from the Declaration of Independence, are on the walls. The memorial is surrounded by Japanese flowering cherry trees. Every spring, the brilliant pink petals of these trees attract thousands of visitors.

The ideals of the American people are also remembered on the Mall. A 50-acre (20-hectare) garden next to the Vietnam Veterans Memorial

The Jefferson Memorial

is dedicated to the Constitution—the document upon which the U.S. government is based. Called Constitution Gardens, the park's flowers, trees, and a peaceful lake make it a popular place to escape the bustling streets of the city.

Most of the monuments stand on the western side of the Mall. On the eastern side, museums have sprouted like mushrooms. The Smithsonian Institution, once just a single building, has grown into a group of sixteen different museums. James Smithson would probably be surprised if he saw them today. The Castle is dwarfed by nine museums that ring the Mall. Other Smithsonian museums have been built in other parts of Washington, D.C., and in New York City. Each of the buildings on the National Mall is devoted to a specific field of study—art, science, nature, history, or technology.

The Lincoln Memorial and the Reflecting Pool (left); Constitution Gardens (right)

Chuck Yeager's Bell X-1 rocket plane

One of the most popular Smithsonian museums is the National Air and Space Museum, which opened in 1976. More than 8 million people crowd through the museum's galleries every year. Visitors see planes that made aviation history hanging from the ceiling—including the first airplane, flown by the Wright Brothers at Kitty Hawk, North Carolina; Charles Lindbergh's *Spirit of St. Louis*; and Chuck Yeager's Bell X-1 rocket plane, the first aircraft to break the sound barrier.

Farther west, the National Museum of Natural History is filled with minerals and animals. People can see the skeleton of an 80-foot (24.4-m) long dinosaur called Diplodicus, or gaze at the Hope Diamond—one of the largest and most beautiful gems in the world. Next door, the National Museum of American History is a treasure trove of historical items. The giant "Star-Spangled Banner" that inspired the U.S. national anthem in 1812 is on display here. Other items in the museum include George Washington's sword, Alexander Graham Bell's telephone, Henry Ford's 1913 Model-T automobile, and gowns of the First Ladies. In an especially popular exhibit, items from movies, television, music, and sports are preserved—including Dorothy's ruby-red slippers from *The Wizard of Oz;* Oscar the Grouch from *Sesame Street;* Michael Jordan's basketball jersey; Muhammad Ali's boxing gloves; and jazzman Dizzy Gillespie's trumpet.

Oscar the Grouch (left) and Dizzy Gillespie's trumpet (below)

Across the Mall from the National Museum of American History stands the Hirshhorn Museum and Sculpture Garden. In this circular building, visitors can see an impressive collection of paintings and sculptures by Rodin, Picasso, Alexander Calder, Mary Cassatt, and Jackson Pollock. Next to the building, seventy-five pieces of sculpture are displayed in an open garden.

Muhammad Ali's boxing gloves

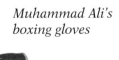

Treasures of all shapes and sizes fill the many museums that make up the Smithsonian Institution. It has been called the "Nation's Attic" because there are millions of objects in its huge collection, and close to a million new items are added every year. Best of all, there is no charge for admission to any of the Smithsonian's museums.

Not all museums on and near the Mall are associated with the Smithsonian. One such museum is the National Gallery of Art. During the 1920s, Andrew W. Mellon, a government official and art collector, made plans for a national art gallery. In 1936, he offered to donate his art collection to the country. One year later, Congress approved money to establish the National Gallery of Art. More money was donated, and construction began. The West Building opened in 1941, and the East Building opened in 1978. Visitors can view works by many famous artists, such as: Leonardo da Vinci, Raphael, Rembrandt, Pierre Auguste Renoir, Georgia O'Keeffe, Winslow Homer, Diego Rivera, and Andy Warhol.

Most of Washington's museums celebrate human achievements, but one museum has been built in memory of humanity's capacity for evil. Just south of the Mall, the United States Holocaust Memorial Museum tells the story of 6 million people who were murdered by the Nazi government of Germany during World War II. Opened in 1993, the museum's exhibits include films, photographs, and objects. Children visiting the museum often see "Daniel's Story: Remember the Children" and "The Children's Wall of Remembrance." Based on the experiences of Jewish families, "Daniel's Story" tells the story of a boy growing up in Nazi Germany during the Holocaust. American schoolchildren contributed to The Children's Wall by painting ceramic tiles. They used this form of artwork to express their feelings about the Holocaust.

The dedication ceremony for the United States Holocaust Memorial Museum on April 22, 1993

An aerial view of one section of "the Quilt"

The United States Holocaust Memorial Museum and other sites around the Mall focus on history. Recent events on the National Mall, however, have called the nation's attention to current issues. During the 1980s, thousands of people began to die of a deadly new disease called AIDS (Acquired Immune Deficiency Syndrome). As in the past, concerned Americans came to the Mall to make the nation aware of an important problem. People from AIDS support groups had created 12-by-12-foot (4-by-4-m) cloth panels, each panel remembering an AIDS victim. They displayed the panels for the first time on October 11, 1987. More than 1,900 panels were spread out over the grass of the Mall, covering an area larger than a football field. These panels are called the NAMES Project AIDS Memorial Quilt, or "the Quilt." When it was laid out again on the Mall in October 1996,

24

the Quilt stretched from the Capitol to the Lincoln Memorial. This time, there were more than 40,000 panels. That showing was the last time the Quilt was displayed in its entirety.

Another issue that troubles Americans is racism. In 1995, African-American leaders asked African-American men from across the nation to assemble on the Mall on October 16. That day, more than 400,000 men met and discussed racism, unemployment, and other problems in their communities. This demonstration, one of the largest in the Mall's history, was called the "Million Man March."

The National Mall during the Million Man March of 1995

As the end of the millennium approached, people considered the Mall the perfect spot to celebrate. On the evening of December 31, 1999, more than 300,000 people gathered between the Lincoln Memorial and Washington Monument. At the stroke of midnight, the frosty night air lit up with a dazzling sound-and-light show that was broadcast throughout the nation.

Along with demonstrations and celebrations, the Mall's monuments are constantly being restored. For more than a hundred years, the Washington Monument had two different shades of stone. Stones used before the Civil War were slightly lighter than those installed after 1878. In the late 1990s, however, workers cleaned the monument, scrubbing and repairing chipped surfaces so that each stone now has the same color.

At the turn of the century, fireworks skyrocket over the Washington Monument.

Fifty American flags, each representing a state, flutter at the monument's base. L'Enfant's dream of a perfect monument at the center of a beautiful city has finally come true.

Demonstrations and restorations of monuments show the important role that the National Mall continues to play in American life. First it was a landscape of empty, rolling fields, and later it became littered with ugly buildings and half-finished projects. Now, the Mall is a beautiful, historic place at the heart of the nation's capital. At the Mall, Americans relax, enjoy the magnificent views, and voice their opinions. The Mall represents the ideals of the United States. Its monuments remind Americans of war veterans, U.S. presidents, and heroic citizens, and its museums open their minds to knowledge, discovery, and beauty.

As one Washington resident said, "the Mall has it all."

Scaffolding surrounds the Washington Monument during its restoration.

FUN FACTS ABOUT

- According to the National Park Service, the most-visited monuments and memorials at the Mall are:

  1) The Vietnam Veterans Memorial

  2) The Franklin Delano Roosevelt Memorial

  3) The Lincoln Memorial

  4) The Korean War Veterans Memorial

  5) The Jefferson Memorial

- It takes most people approximately one hour to walk (without stopping) the length of the Mall (from the Capitol to the Lincoln Memorial).

- The Mall is almost two miles long and a quarter of a mile wide.

- The National Park Service estimates that approximately 5 million people visit the National Mall every year. About seventy park rangers work there every day between 8:00 A.M. and midnight.

- When it was completed in 1884, the Washington Monument was the tallest structure in the world. Five years later, the Eiffel Tower in Paris, France, became the tallest structure.

- The elevator in the Washington Monument goes from the bottom to the top in seventy seconds.

THE NATIONAL MALL

- The statue of Abraham Lincoln in the Lincoln Memorial is made of twenty-eight blocks of white marble.

- More than 6,000 tons of granite (enough to erect an eighty-story building) were used in the construction of the Franklin Delano Roosevelt Memorial. The largest stone in the memorial measures 21 feet (6.4 m) long by 6 feet (1.83 m) high.

- In 1912, the city of Tokyo gave the city of Washington, D.C., three thousand Japanese flowering cherry trees. These trees, which bloom in late March and early April, now surround the Tidal Basin, a pool near the Potomac River and the Thomas Jefferson Memorial. More than fifty years later, Japan donated 3,800 more trees to beautify the city.

- During the construction of the Vietnam Veterans Memorial, visitors began leaving objects— from birthday cards to wreaths— near the names of loved ones who died during the Vietnam War. Rangers at the National Park Service collect these items, and most of them are saved in the Vietnam Veterans Memorial Collection. People continue to leave items at the Wall every day. Two of the most popular days to leave objects in memory of Vietnam veterans are Memorial Day and Veterans Day.

GLOSSARY

Pierre Charles L'Enfant was an architect.

architect – a person who designs buildings and oversees their construction

assemble – to bring together as a group

battlement – a low, protective wall built along the top of a castle or fort; battlements have openings for soldiers to shoot through

capital – a city where a state or national government is located

Capitol – the building where the U.S. Congress meets

citizen – a person who is an official member of a political body, such as a country

civil rights – the rights that every member of a society has to freedom and equal treatment under the law

demonstration – a display of public feeling, as in a rally or a parade

gallery – a group of rooms where artworks or historical items are exhibited

granite – a hard rock that is used in buildings and monuments

Holocaust – total destruction and great loss of life; the Nazi murder of 6 million Jews is called "the Holocaust"

landscape – to make a piece of land more beautiful by planting trees, shrubs, and flowers; land considered scenic

marble – a limestone that can be highly polished and used for buildings and sculptures

Nazis – members of a group that controlled Germany from 1933 to 1945 under the leadership of Adolf Hitler

obelisk – tall pillar

panel – a piece that forms part of a wall or other surface

protest – a strong objection

veterans – people who have served their country in war

The Washington Monument is an obelisk.

TIMELINE

1791 Congress hires L'Enfant to design capital city

1848

Smithsonian Institution opens **1855**

American Civil War { **1861**
1865

Washington Monument completed **1884**

McMillan Plan calls for Mall to be restored **1902**

Construction begins on Washington Monument

1922 Lincoln Memorial dedicated

1937 Congress establishes National Gallery of Art

1939

1943 Jefferson Memorial dedicated

Marian Anderson performs at Lincoln Memorial

1963 *August 28:* Martin Luther King Jr.'s "I Have a Dream" speech

1976 National Air and Space Museum opens

1982 Vietnam Veterans Memorial dedicated

1987 *October 11:* First showing of the Quilt

1993

Vietnam Women's Memorial and U.S. Holocaust Memorial Museum dedicated

Korean War Veterans Memorial dedicated; Million Man March takes place

1995

1997 Franklin Delano Roosevelt Memorial dedicated

1999 *December 31:* Sound-and-light show celebrated millennium

INDEX (*Boldface* *page numbers indicate illustrations.*)

PHOTO CREDITS

Photographs ©: Andrew H. MacDonald: 9, 31 top; AP/Wide World Photos: 1, 3, 23, 31 bottom, cover (Charles Pereira/U.S. Park Service); Art Resource, NY: 8 (National Portrait Gallery, Smithsonian Institution); Corbis-Bettmann: 16, 28 (Bruce Burkhardt), 19 (Patrick Ward); Jay Mallin: 25; Liaison Agency, Inc.: 26 (Mark Wilson); Library of Congress: 6, 30 top; Mae Scanlan: 11, 17, 18, 20, 21, 27, 30 bottom; Naval Historical Foundation: 12 (National Archives); New England Stock Photo: 15 (Andre Jenny), 14, 29 (Margo Taussig Pinkerton); North Wind Picture Archives: 7; Photo Researchers: 24 (Linda Bartlett); Stock Montage, Inc.: 10, 13 bottom, 31 center; Tom Dietrich: 2, 13 top. Map by TJS Design.

PICTURE IDENTIFICATIONS

Cover: Aerial view of a section of the National Mall—from the Washington Monument to the Capitol—during the Million Man March on October 16, 1995
Page 1: Marian Anderson performs on the steps of the Lincoln Memorial on April 9, 1939.
Page 2: On the Fourth of July, crowds gather on the National Mall to await the annual fireworks display.

ABOUT THE AUTHOR

Brendan January was born and raised in Pleasantville, New York. He is a graduate of Haverford College and the Columbia Graduate School of Journalism. An American history enthusiast, he has written several books for Children's Press, including *The Emancipation Proclamation, Fort Sumter, The Dred Scott Decision, The Lincoln-Douglas Debates,* and *The Assassination of Abraham Lincoln.* January's *Science in the Renaissance* was chosen by the Children's Book Council as an Outstanding Science Trade Book. He is a journalist for the *Philadelphia Inquirer,* and he lives in New Jersey.